# SHAKESPEARE
## AND HIS WORLD

### IVOR BROWN

*Author of "Shakespeare", "How
Shakespeare Spent the Day", etc.*

LUTTERWORTH PRESS · LONDON

*First published 1964*

# Acknowledgements

THE Publishers wish to thank the following for permission to reproduce photographs of which they hold the copyright. (The numbers refer to the pages on which they appear.) The Marquis of Salisbury and The Courtauld Institute of Art [2]; National Portrait Gallery [5, 9 (left), 12 (right), 13, 39, 42 (lower)]; Radio Times Hulton Picture Library [6, 25 (upper), 33, 35, 36]; The Trustees of the Victoria and Albert Museum [7 (upper), 8, 15 (left), 31 (left), 32, 37]; The London Museum [7 (lower), 14 (right), 15 (right), 27, 29, 42 (top), 55]; The Trustees of the National Maritime Museum [9 (right), 10, 11, 12 (left)]; Thomas Photos, Oxford [14 (left)]; the Bodleian Library, Oxford [14 (left), 40]; B. T. Batsford Ltd. [16]; Country Life Ltd. [17, 18]; J. Allan Cash [19]; Jarrold and Sons Ltd. and The Trustees of the Shakespeare Birthplace Trust [20, 21, 22, 24, 25 (lower)]; The Trustees of the British Museum [23 (right), 28, 30, 36 (lower), 43, 44]; Henry E. Huntington Library and Art Gallery, California [26, 31 (right)]; Dulwich College [34]; The Faculty of Music and the University Press, Oxford [38]; British Travel and Holidays Association and The Trustees of the Shakespeare Birthplace Trust [41]; and The Wellcome Historical Medical Museum [46, 47].

The photograph on the back of the jacket shows Anne Hathaway's cottage at Shottery, and is reproduced by permission of Jarrold and Sons Ltd. and The Trustees of the Shakespeare Birthplace Trust.

*Printed in Great Britain
by The Camelot Press Ltd.,
London and Southampton*

*The portrait of Shakespeare that has a strong claim to be an authentic contemporary likeness. Tradition assigned it to the hand of Richard Burbage.*

WILLIAM SHAKESPEARE was born in April, 1564, and died in April, 1616. He had risen quickly in the theatre as actor and author and had a profitable share in management by the time that he was thirty. He soon had made enough money to become the owner of the chief house in his birthplace, the country town of Stratford-upon-Avon in Warwickshire. The background of his career was the England of Queen Elizabeth. His plays throw light on it and are also more easily understood if we know the way of life in the England and the London of that period.

His fame has spread so widely and has risen so high that we may think of him as a very important person in his own lifetime. That he was not. The actors were under the protection of the Court and of some noblemen who enjoyed the entertainment which they provided. Without that protection they could not have acted at all and Shakespeare might have been driven into some other profession. For play-acting was despised and even hated by many prominent citizens in the merchant class of the City of London who regarded the theatre as a sinful place and the players as corrupters of the people. The increasing number of religious Puritans would have prohibited the making and perform-ance of plays. Fortunately the Court could prevent that and of course many of the poorer citizens as well as some of the rich loved going to the theatre. The theatrical profession depended for its existence on royal and aristocratic protection and its members had no great social standing. In Shakespeare's home-town, which had welcomed visiting players in his younger days, there was a growing desire to keep them out. Some of his neighbours must have looked sourly at the retired dramatist who had made his money in what they called "the devil's work-shop".

5

*Nothing travelled faster than the speed of the horse. This is part of a sixteenth-century engraving showing a German riverside city.*

We must not be dazzled by the blaze of glory which later surrounded the poet's name into thinking of England as full of Shakespeare-worship in his lifetime. If an important Elizabethan statesman like Lord Burghley had been told that he would be remembered only in history-books while Shakespeare's plays were everywhere so much read, acted, and admired that his name was familiar to the whole world, he could not have believed this for a moment. People of to-day have expressed surprise that his death did not immediately evoke nation-wide tributes and was not followed by the general mourning and impressive funeral in Westminster Abbey which followed the death of Charles Dickens two and a half centuries later. This shows some ignorance of the way of life in Elizabethan times. Communications were slow and scanty to a degree inconceivable by the young people of to-day who take the immediate supply of news from all over the world for granted. In Shakespeare's time news travelled at the speed of a horse, if a horseman was available.

Shakespeare died on April 23, and was buried two days later in his parish church beside the Avon. Stratford is nearly a hundred miles from London and, had a rider set out with the news in order to inform his fellow-actors at their theatres, he would have reached them when the funeral was over. For the sad fact to be known outside London would have taken far longer. Shakespeare's England had a loneliness of which we know nothing. To understand his life and his plays we have to imagine a world immensely different from our own.

It was a world, for example, in which distance was a real and formidable thing. Within as small a country as Britain there could be great isolations. The sailors and

6

explorers showed much daring and resource, but their voyages took months and years to cover oceans now crossed by aeroplane in a few hours. The rate of travel was to remain the same for another two hundred years. When Charles Dickens was born in 1812 people were travelling no faster and getting news no quicker than the ancient Greeks and Romans had done; their transport and communications were limited to the pace of the sailing-ship, the horse, and the human foot. Our modern inventions during the last century and a half have virtually abolished distance and separation.

These inventions have given us many comforts and a standard of health undreamed of by the people of Shakespeare's time. I am not forgetting our discomforts of noise and overcrowding. But it is a fair guess that few now would prefer the old way of existence, with its primitive medicine, its absence of dentistry and sanitation, its scourge of death-dealing plague, its cruelties and savage penal system, and its long winter nights whose darkness had to be fought with feeble rush-lights (candles were far from cheap) and oil-lamps or the carrying of torches. The winter diet was monotonous and unhealthy since meat and fish could only be preserved by salting, vegetables were scarce, and scurvy was the commonest of diseases. We have canning and refrigeration and the importation of fruits as well as meat from far and wide. The world is at our doors and in our larders, and we are healthier for it.

*Dessert trenchers were used as plates at Elizabethan dinner parties. They were decorated on the reverse side with designs and inscriptions, sometimes for amusement. This one depicts a lawyer.*

Merry England is a phrase of modern usage. It creates the idea of a land of plenty in which everybody had a song in his heart with abundance on his plate and a tankard at his lips. There is some truth in that picture. There was less tension because there was less drive and competition in industry. The workers were still mainly craftsmen who could take a personal interest in their job and were not assembled in masses to do routine work in mills and factories with possibly long and crowded journeys to and from the office and workshop. There was much worse to come when steam-power and machinery

*A place at table as set c. 1600. The earthenware dishes and mugs are glazed in yellow or black; the spoon is pewter; there is no fork.*

brought about a revolution in industry and harsh employers could enforce appalling conditions of labour even on the children who were sent into the mines as well as the mills. To read a play of Shakespeare's time such as *The Shoemaker's Holiday* and follow it up with Dickens' *Hard Times*, a story of factory life in Northern England, is to realize the disastrous change in a labouring family's life.

Merry England was not a myth, despite the material limitations, but it was Darkest England when the epidemics killed people by the thousand. Shakespeare's contemporary, Thomas Dekker, who wrote *The Shoemaker's Holiday*, also wrote a description of the plague in London which presents the other side of the Elizabethan picture with merciless and terrifying detail. Shakespeare himself has also shown most vividly the contrasts of gaiety and gloom. His comedies present a world that is living "on top of happy hours". His tragedies reveal the crimes and cruelties of men and the sins of society. It is true that the scene of his comedies is usually set in foreign countries and in earlier ages. But the dates and places are inessential. He was writing of what he saw and felt amid the humours and horrors of the life around him, now with laughter, now with loathing. The whole image of his period is there, although the happiness may be set in Italy or Illyria and the despair portrayed in the vanished worlds of King Lear's England or Macbeth's Scotland.

So in order to understand Shakespeare and his surroundings we must not only view his England as entirely different from to-day's in habits and amenities; we must

*A superb example of Elizabethan embroidery depicting a country scene.*

The two sovereigns who reigned during Shakespeare's lifetime. Queen Elizabeth I and King James VI of Scotland who became James I of England.

also view it with a sense of proportion, balancing the better with the worse. It is fair to begin by looking at the bright side and turn later to the shadows and the darkness.

There was peace in the land, if not outside it. During the previous century England had been torn by civil war; the armies of York and Lancaster who marched and counter-marched across the country in the lengthy Wars of the Roses were small by modern reckoning, but there was no security for the farmers and peasants over whose land they ranged in search of supplies while they fought their many and bloody battles. The Lancastrian victory at the battle of Bosworth Field in 1483 and the firm establishment of the Tudor monarchy had put an end to the vicious brawling of contentious barons, and to the hatred and chaos in which Englishmen had slaughtered Englishmen and fathers had fought with sons. About many of Shakespeare's opinions there can be doubt; but certainly he appreciated and vehemently supported the presence of a strong monarchy which at last could hold the nation together. His historical plays continually repeat the necessity of an ordered life with discipline enforced upon the powerful and quarrelsome great families by a still more powerful king or queen. The final message in his early play of *King John*

Naught shall make us rue
If England to itself do rest but true

is always being sounded until in his very late play of *King Henry VIII* he gives prophetic praise to the peace and security of Queen Elizabeth's reign, in which

9

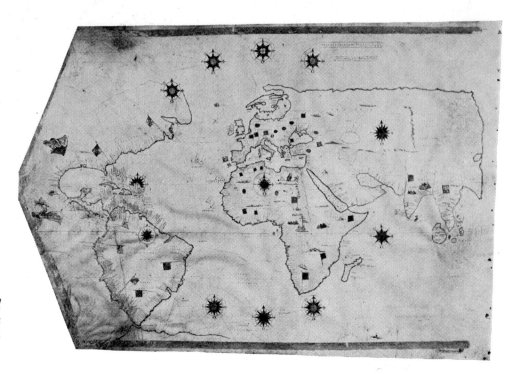

*A map of the world c. 1540. The coast of Africa is fairly accurate, but much of the world is unknown.*

> Every man shall eat in safety,
> Under his own vine, what he plants, and sing
> The merry songs of peace to all his neighbours.

The horrors of civil war were to be suffered again only a quarter of a century after Shakespeare's death; but the sixteenth and early seventeenth centuries had been spared them. Here was one good reason for relief and for rejoicing.

The bitter strife between the Roman Catholics and Protestants was not abolished in Queen Elizabeth's reign, but a settlement had been imposed and the Church of England firmly established. Persecution did not cease, but at least it was diminished. Three years after her death in 1603 and the succession of King James the First, the failure of the Gunpowder Plot put an end to the scheming and occasional insurrections of the more fanatical devotees of the Old Religion. It had become much easier for a man minding his own business "under his own vine" to live a peaceful family life and go about his work with confidence.

That was a tremendous gain, and the nation as the years went by realized the value of strong central government personified in the magnetic personality of the Virgin Queen, the strength and splendour of whose reign won her the title of Gloriana. We need not here go into the complexities of her character. Hot-tempered, extravagant, and capricious she might sometimes be, but she had brought not only peace at home, but

10

victory at sea. Her sailors had beaten off the Spanish menace, defeating the great Armada in 1588. Before long they were strong enough (daring they never lacked) to sail into the enemy's harbour of Cadiz in 1596 and successfully destroy the new Armada being prepared for a further assault on England. Across the Irish Channel there was hostility still, but the Union of the Crowns under King James ended the threat of the bitter wars with Scotland which had so long brought havoc and massacre to both sides of the Border.

Peace could not be total at home and abroad. The rebellious spirit is strong in mankind. But a great measure of security and tranquillity had been achieved.

> Our children's children
> Shall see this and bless heaven.

Thus wrote Shakespeare in the speech already quoted. He spoke, it is true, as the dramatist of the King's Men,

*Sir Francis Drake (1540?–96) who circumnavigated the world in his ship the Golden Hind in 1577–81. He was one of the commanders of the English fleet which defeated the Spanish Armada in 1588.*

*Drake's dial, and details of its various parts, which include a table of compass bearings of the moon, an equatorial dial, a perpetual calendar, a table of latitudes, a dial for finding the time of high water, and another for showing the course of the sun through the signs of the Zodiac, phases of the moon and aspects of the planets.*

The Golden Lion, *a ship of c. 1588.*

*Sir Walter Raleigh (1552?–1618), explorer, historian, courtier, poet and wit, with his son. A portrait painted in 1602.*

players attached to the Court, who had to say the tactful thing; but here he spoke for the people too. He was one of them, confident that in his time no civil war would bring an insurgent army trampling over his Stratford acres.

The sailors were also explorers. They could not, of course, defeat distance in the way that we have done. They could not go fast, but they could and did go far. While Shakespeare was still at school, Francis Drake was the first Englishman to sail round the world. He had already made two successful crossings to the West Indies, more for the purpose of capturing Spanish vessels carrying rich cargoes than of adding to the map. In 1577 this brilliant navigator from Devonshire began the great voyage of the *Golden Hind*, which lasted four years; the Portuguese Admiral Magellan had been before him in rounding the extreme tip of South America, whose stormy straits have perpetuated his name. But he did not come back alive. Drake rounded Cape Horn, crossed the Pacific and Indian oceans, and reached Plymouth once more by way of South Africa. When we think of the tiny size of his ship and all the difficulties of keeping enough food and water on board, such feats of endurance and seamanship are astounding.

It was search for power and wealth rather than desire for knowledge that impelled the adventurers, who were pirates as well as patriots. Gold was more than geography to Queen Elizabeth, but inevitably the victorious captains learned as they looted. One man of intellect as well as daring to carry on the penetration of the Indies and South America was Sir Walter Raleigh. He also came from the West of England; he was a courtier, a dandy, and a poet who could face immense hardships in his efforts to discover in Guiana the fabled El Dorado or Land of Gold. Shakespeare's play, *The Tempest*, is a wonderful work of fancy, but it is based on fact and on the records of Sir George Somers, who was wrecked on the Bermudas and managed to make his return in 1610. Somers was Admiral of the Virginia Company, which had been formed to explore and exploit the southern coast of North America.

The seafarers had the financial backing of the Queen and of men of wealth who had greater wealth in view, but we must not think of them as get-rich-quick speculators. They were men of taste who were as ready to support the production of plays and poetry as they were to put their money in a voyage to El Dorado. The Earl of Southampton was Shakespeare's patron; he was also a member of the Virginia Company. Raleigh applied a masterly use of English to his unfinished *History of the World* as well as to his poems.

That was characteristic of the Elizabethan age.

*Phineas Pett (1570–1647), a shipwright who became the Masterbuilder of the Navy. He built the* Prince Royal *(launched in 1610), which can be seen in the inset of this portrait, which was the largest ship ever built at that period.*

Its young men had fine language on their lips and were as ready with a sonnet as with a sword. They had restless, darting minds and a keen sense of beauty. They were foppish and extravagantly fond of jewels and rich costumes. But they had no fear, and were reckless in politics as in war and hazardous enterprise. To offend the Queen in her last years of imperious majesty meant disgrace and imprisonment and possibly death. One of them, the Earl of Essex, even raised a rebellion and died for it. They lived in gaiety and danger, and went handsomely dressed to the executioner's block; their sense of showmanship was strong even to the most gruesome end.

Whether death came from the Spaniard, a fatal storm at sea, or an accusation of treason at home, they had a flourish and phrase to meet it. This was shown in their last words: "We are as near to heaven by sea as by land." "What dost thou fear? Strike, man, strike." These fiery spirits could have stayed comfortably on their estates and shared the peace that the common people were enjoying under the firm Elizabethan rule. But tranquillity bored them. And so the reign had its two great contrasts. There was a settled country. But many of its greatest countrymen were too ambitious and too eager for brave undertakings to settle down. Among other famous sailors and explorers were Sir Humphrey

*Sir Martin Frobisher (1535?–94), the explorer, painted by Cornelius Ketelin in 1577, wearing sea-dress.*

*The blouse and breeches of coarse linen worn by seamen and London watermen of the sixteenth century.*

Gilbert, Sir Martin Frobisher, and Sir Richard Grenville. As early as 1575 Gilbert wrote a *Discourse on the North West Passage to India* to suggest that it was possible to get round the north of America as well as south by Cape Horn. He tried to do so in vain, but later he occupied Newfoundland in the Queen's name and founded the first British colony. He was drowned on the way home when his little frigate, the *Squirrel*, was overturned in a gale.

Frobisher attempted the North West Passage three times and made adventurous voyages to Africa, the West Indies, and Asia Minor. He was very successful in naval warfare and commanded a ship, the *Triumph*, when the Spanish Armada was routed. Grenville was another indomitable fighter. He was made famous for ever by Lord Tennyson's ballad about the *Revenge*. In this ship in 1591, off "Flores in the Azores", he engaged a Spanish fleet of fifty-three vessels and continued the madly uneven combat until, as Raleigh reported, all the decks, masts, and tackle had gone and there was only "the very foundation of a ship, nothing being left over-head either for fight or defence". Before his gallant end he had been with Raleigh to the coast of Virginia. In tiny ships and in unknown waters they took their lives in their hands and were ready for all risks.

*A miniature painting by Nicholas Hilliard, c. 1588, of an Eliza-◄ bethan gentleman.*

*Late sixteenth-century costume including doublet and hose, hat, ▶ gloves and short cloak.*

*Arlington Row, Bibury. A famous old street in the Cotswolds country with which Shakespeare was familiar.*

The voyages brought money in, and not only from the Golden West. English trade was expanding into Europe and eastward along the Mediterranean shores and beyond. Hence came the spices with which the Elizabethans loved to flavour their diet and some of the costly materials for their elegant costumes. A nation has to export to pay for its imports and England had a great source of wealth in its sheep and their wool. Those who travel about England to-day and look for old towns where buildings of the sixteenth and seventeenth centuries remain will discover them in counties famous for their flocks. One of these areas, the Cotswolds of Gloucestershire, was close to Stratford-upon-Avon and here the farmers and the landlords throve and had money to build their beautiful manor-houses of the soft-tinted local stone. They were grateful to God and spent freely on their magnificent churches in which they employed sculptors to make their handsome and imposing tombs. In Suffolk, another sheep-county, the churches are often of a tremendous size, far beyond the needs of the parish but evidence of riches and of a devoted pride in the use of them.

The homes of the great landowners in the Middle Ages had been castles. The Normans who came in with William the Conqueror were invaders who had to protect themselves. Their descendants were quarrelsome and fought each other. There was no internal peace in the land until the end of the fifteenth century, when the Wars of the Roses were ended and the comparative tranquillity of the Tudor times began. Then the need for a rich man's house that was also a fortress diminished and it was possible to plan for comfortable habitation instead of for defence. Visitors to Stratford-upon-Avon

16

*Hardwick Hall, a magnificent example of the new Elizabethan architecture. It was built in 1590–97 by Elizabeth, Countess of Shrewsbury, whose initials can be seen in the stone balustrade.* (Country Life photo.)

will probably also be taken to the noble ruins of Kenilworth Castle. This had once been occupied by Lord Leicester, a favourite at Queen Elizabeth's Court. Here in 1575 he entertained her lavishly with pageantry and performances in his grounds, and it is likely that Shakespeare as a boy of eleven was taken to see the plays and masquerades and to hear the music, of which a description has been left.

The great castles were not needed by the new rich. They must have been extremely hard to keep warm and well-lit, and fortresses, naturally, do not have large windows to let in the light. Their windows are slits which a bowman could use should the enemy approach. It is significant that when a new mansion was built in this reign—Hardwick Hall in Derbyshire—it was designed with as many and as large windows as possible to

*A bedroom in Hardwick Hall, showing a four-poster bed and other furniture of the period. (Country Life photo.)*

*The Gallery at Hardwick Hall, the walls of which are still hung with contemporary tapestries. Such galleries were a special feature of large Elizabethan houses and were used for walking exercise in bad weather. (Country Life photo.)*

catch what sun the climate may provide. Also the front door was flat on the ground and so easy to enter and there were fine, broad staircases. In a castle the way from one storey to another is usually a steep, narrow stairway. From the top of it defenders can easily beat back the hostile intruder. Large windows and broad stairs are signs of confidence. The enemy is not expected.

During and just after Shakespeare's time the sense of security allowed those with money for building to forget about moats and drawbridges, turrets and vantage-points for archery or musketry. The Cotswold manor-houses of the squires, who were growing fat on their mutton and the sale of wool, are domestic, not defensive—not cumbrous, like castles, but natural homes for law-abiding folk. Being made of native material they seem to grow naturally out of the ground and not to be dumped upon it, and so they are examples of fine architecture as well as history written in stone.

Francis Bacon, who began to write his famous *Essays* at the end of Elizabeth's reign, started his essay on Buildings, with the simple statement, "Houses are built to live in". That seems absurdly obvious to us. But it would not have been obvious to a medieval nobleman who wanted a stronghold in which to keep alive. Bacon followed

*Moreton Old Hall, Cheshire. A typical example of the ornate design and timbering achieved in Elizabethan houses. The moat was retained for its appearance and not for protection.*

this piece with another on Gardens, and to think much about and to spend much on lawns and flower-beds shows a further reliance upon peaceful times. In the devising both of houses and gardens, Bacon was thinking of owners who could plan on princely lines, but everywhere over England there was opportunity now for men of lesser means to establish themselves in comfortable, unfortified dwellings, and to take much thought about their flowers, trees and shrubs.

They had a fine taste for landscape-gardening and liked what was called topiary— that is clipping and trimming shrubs into fantastic and ornamental shapes. Alleys ran among the patterned hedges and these pleasant places Shakespeare had in mind in his garden or orchard scenes, when the plot involved hiding and over-hearing. The great gardens also provided herbs for use in medicines.

*Mary Arden's house contains a fascinating farming museum that includes implements going back to Shakespeare's time.*

*The farmhouse home of Mary Arden, Shakespeare's mother, at Wilmcote, near Stratford.*

Building, of course, varies according to the material at hand. In counties where stone was easily available, that was used with stone tiles for the roof. Elsewhere flint and brick, often timbered, provided the general method of construction with thatch on top. Gables were common. Anne Hathaway's cottage at Shottery, close to Stratford, is typical of a farmer's house in Shakespeare's time. His mother's family, the Ardens, lived nearby at Wilmcote, and theirs was a larger place. Both can be visited, and have been well preserved. As specimens of the country-town house of a prosperous man, there are in Stratford both Shakespeare's birthplace and the home of Dr. John Hall, who was a prominent local physician, and married Shakespeare's daughter, Susanna. All these include specimens of the furniture of the period, and the two farmhouses show the kind of implements and gear employed in domestic work and on the land.

A conspicuous feature of a Tudor farm was the dovecot. This could be very large; one had six hundred nesting-holes. The reason for that was the use of pigeons for food, especially in the late winter and spring, when meat was running short. The dovecot made a handsome addition to the farmyard. Another provider of food lay in the fish-ponds. These were of good service to the religious houses, where the monks had to abstain from meat during their fasts.

*The living-room of Anne Hathaway's cottage, showing the open hearth and, on the right, the old wooden settee on which, according to tradition, Anne Hathaway and William Shakespeare may have sat while courting.*

Furnishing was of a simple kind even in a royal home. A courtier complained of the hard stools in the palace of Whitehall. A few of the richest people had carpets. The common practice was to strew dried rushes on the floor. There were also plaited rush mats. Painted cloths were hung on the walls quite commonly and these were not expensive; elaborate tapestries and framed pictures were the decorations only in the homes of the noblemen. Oak-panelling was used where oak was plentiful, but it was considered a luxury and used up the wood needed for the oak tables, chairs, and stools of the ordinary home. We know from records in people's wills that in Shakespeare's time the labourers had their painted cloths, often showing Biblical scenes, in their bedrooms as well as sitting-rooms.

The four-poster beds of the prosperous were made with handsomely carved "testers", or roofs, and with side-pillars. The mattresses were made of rushes and placed on a network of strong cords. The Elizabethans did not sleep as comfortably as we do, even in the wealthy houses, and the servants and children had to make do with truckle-beds. These were very low on the ground and could be stowed away under the big four-posters, which were known as standing-beds. If people did not lie soft, those in a standing-bed could keep warm by drawing the curtains round them and by inserting warming-pans, their substitute for our safer hot-water bottles. Solid oak coffers were useful for storing bedclothes and other textiles.

The structure of furniture is more likely to be preserved than its upholstery.

22

Shakespeare and his family must have been used to sitting hard if their chairs were no more covered than as we see them now. The narrow, upright uncushioned settee in Anne Hathaway's cottage at Shottery does not look a cosy place for courting.

In a workaday household the food was eaten off wooden plates or trenchers. But a prosperous farmer would have some pewter dishes. Silver or even gold was to be found in the dinner-service of a big house or a palace, and there too forks would be found. But these were only coming in during Shakespeare's lifetime and to have them was at first regarded as a foreign habit. There were knives and spoons and probably much use of the fingers which were washed by those with cleanly ideas in handy bowls of water. In the poor homes drinking vessels were of wood or horn, and the bottles for the beer were made of leather. The name of voiders was given to vessels in which the scraps were thrown away. The references in Shakespeare's plays to orts (scraps of food left over) show that he hated the sight of the greasy remains of a meal and dirty utensils, while he was very conscious of bad smells.

The methods of making glass had been known for centuries, but, when it was expensive and hard to come by, it was naturally not much used by common people, even if they could get it, because it is so easily broken and then the money spent on it is wasted. We must remember that all goods brought to the countryside had a slow journey in a cart over rough roads and glass would have to be very carefully packed to survive the transport, especially if it first came from abroad. Venetian glass, as it was called, was being imported and imitated in London during Elizabeth's reign. But it was not for humble people. They would sing, "Troll, troll, the jolly nut-brown bowl," if they were having a party.

The agricultural implements were simple. The earth was still sometimes turned by

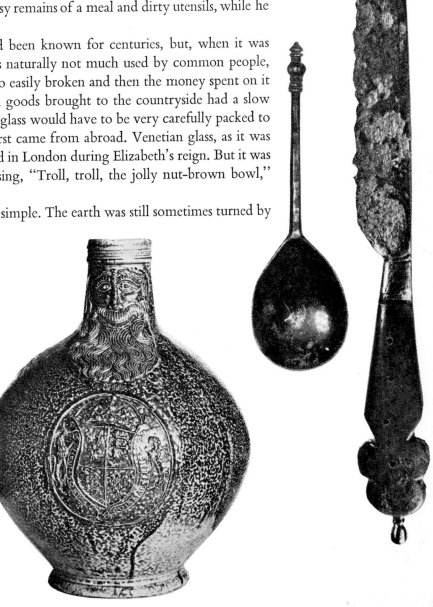

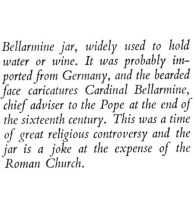

*Bellarmine jar, widely used to hold water or wine. It was probably imported from Germany, and the bearded face caricatures Cardinal Bellarmine, chief adviser to the Pope at the end of the sixteenth century. This was a time of great religious controversy and the jar is a joke at the expense of the Roman Church.*

a lonely peasant pushing a breast-plough, but a good farm with labourers has its team of oxen for yoking to the plough. This was mostly made of wood, but had an iron tip for cutting through the soil. Ploughing with oxen could be sometimes seen in the Cotswold in our own century. The people of Europe admired the breeds of cattle on the farms of Elizabethan England. Of the oxen it was written: "They will plough in tough clay and upon hilly ground where horses of an indifferent goodness will stand still."

Crops had to be cut with scythes and sickles and the grain thrashed out with a flail. It was all gruelling hand labour which Shakespeare remembered when he wrote in *The Tempest*:

Ye sun-burned sicklemen of August weary.

He mentioned the hats made of rye straw, which protected them from the sun. The weary ones would go home to their nut-brown bowls and rush mattresses, with the prospect of more hard work with the flail to follow. What would they have thought of a modern, motor-driven combined harvester?

*The kitchen of a typical Tudor homestead, with some of the cooking equipment of the period.*

*Sowing and harrowing. An illustration from the ballad, "The countryman's going sowing in the countrie", c. 1589.*

*The finely-carved late Elizabethan bedstead that belonged to the Hathaway family. The mattress is of rush supported on cords threaded through the wooden frame.*

*A street-seller with hand screens for protecting ladies' faces from the heat of the open fire. An engraving from* The Manner of Crying Things in London, *1599 (?)*

The Elizabethan prosperity was reflected in the growth of the English capital. The number of its people is not exactly known because there was no census taken then, but it is calculated that when the Queen came to the throne London had a population of one hundred thousand and that when she died it was twice as many. Now a single London suburb, Hampstead, for example, has a hundred thousand inhabitants and the huge and ever-growing urban region of Greater London will soon contain ten millions.

There is a pictorial view of London made in 1600 which gives us a good idea of the town to which Shakespeare came as a young man seeking a career with the players. The Thames was broader and in parts more shallow than it is now because embankments have been made to tidy it up. There was only one bridge, the famous London Bridge, and this was also a street with quite big houses on it. To the north of this was the City, on the site of the old Roman settlement; here lived the merchants, very serious people who would not allow play-acting

26

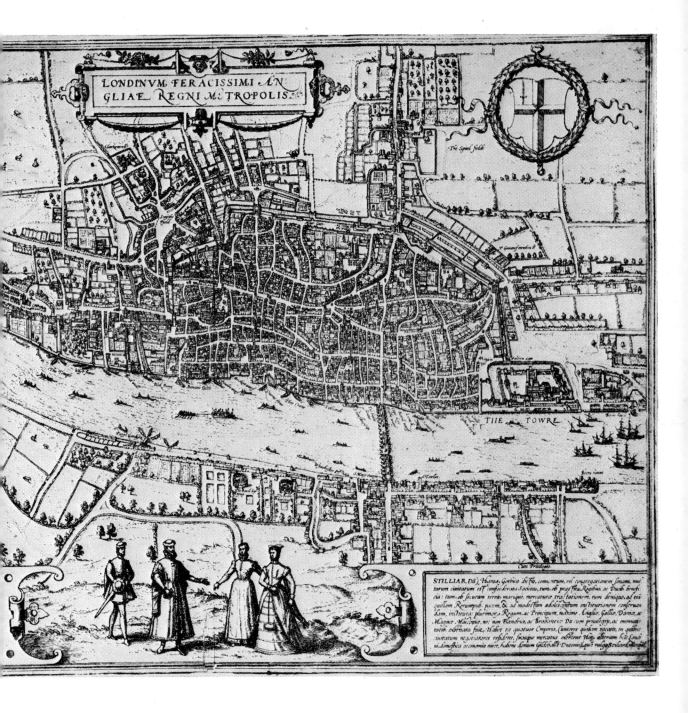

*A map of London attributed to J. Hoefnagel, showing the City (above) and Westminster (on the far left) at the time of the accession of Elizabeth I in 1558. Notice the Thames, only spanned by one bridge, London Bridge, with its busy traffic of all types of vessels.*

In the foreground is a view of Bankside where Shakespeare lived for many years, showing the Bear Garden and a theatre to which the name of *The Globe* is given. That was the scene of Shakespeare's greatest triumphs. And for a while he lodged in this district. On the north banks stand St. Paul's Cathedral and many other medieval churches, destroyed in the Great Fire of 1666.

within their boundaries. Their rule ended where the River Fleet joined the Thames at what is now Ludgate Circus; the Fleet had been a navigable stream, with ships sailing up to what is now Holborn. Now it is a drain covered over and running under Farringdon Street. In Shakespeare's time it was much fouled because there were no regular drains, and people threw out their garbage into what was called the Fleet Ditch.

West of the Fleet, the citizens were free of the City's discipline, and there was a theatre in Blackfriars and others away to the north, where this new business of building playhouses had begun in 1575 in the suburb of Shoreditch. If we imagine a journey westward along the Strand, originally La Straunde, we would pass the Inns of Court,

then as now the haunt of the lawyers, and the great London houses of the noblemen. These stretched down to the river, and had water-gates above the moorings where they kept their stately barges. Much of London's travel was then made by water. The titles of the owners of these riverside mansions are still preserved in the London street-names of Essex, Arundel, Norfolk and Northumberland.

That brings us to Whitehall where was the principal palace; in it we know that performances of Shakespeare's plays were given by royal command. And so to Westminster with its Abbey and Hall, two of the few buildings that have survived from Elizabethan London. The town was clustered close to the river and did not stretch at all far inland. Gerard, a famous writer about flowers and plants, mentioned gathering herbs "on the banks of Pickadilla"; so what is now Piccadilly was then quite rural. The curious name came from the country house built by a merchant of pickadills, the huge lace ruffs which fashionable people wore round their necks. It was nicknamed Pickadilla Hall. There was a windmill where the Windmill Theatre is now.

The south bank of the Thames was outside the City, and so it could be used for purposes forbidden in the City. Theatres were built there in what is now the Borough of Southwark, and there too was Paris Garden, with its bear-pits. A famous actor called Alleyn ran the Garden at a large profit and probably made far more money in this way than he did by acting. But he put his fortune to good use by founding a college at Dulwich. This shore of the Thames became London's chief pleasure-ground and had many famous inns. Shakespeare himself lodged there for some years, but moved across the river later, perhaps to find a quieter place.

All towns are made noisy now by the ceaseless motor traffic. But they were not quiet then. There was a great deal of bell-ringing, with peals to tell the time of day or night as well as the hours of church

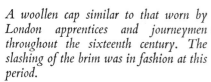

*A woollen cap similar to that worn by London apprentices and journeymen throughout the sixteenth century. The slashing of the brim was in fashion at this period.*

*A barber's and a shoemaker's shop. There was shampooing in Shakespeare's time, but that word, which originally meant massaging, came in, probably from India, much later.*

services. There was a gloomy funeral bell to announce a death, and its frequent booming added to the horrors of the plague years. The streets were narrow, and crowded with vehicles of all kinds. Thomas Dekker has told of the uproar and crowding in the narrow lanes:

"Carts and coaches make such a thundering din as if the world ran on wheels; at every corner men, women, and children meet in such shoals that posts are set up to strengthen the houses lest with jostling with one another they should shoulder them down. Besides, hammers are beating in one place, tubs hooping in another, pots clinking in a third, water-tankards running at tilt in a fourth. . . . Tradesmen, as if they were dancing galliards, are lusty at legs and never stand still."

Evidently there is nothing new in the rush and strain of town life. A Swiss traveller, who was rowed across the Thames to see a play about Julius Caesar (almost certainly Shakespeare's) in 1599, has left a vivid description of the busy town and its bustling markets. Rest was taken, he said, in the many taverns with their gardens, which were very popular and full of women as well as of men. But here too there was no tranquillity, because music was provided, and the hostelry where he stayed was visited by various kinds of performers every day.

He was much struck by the number of boats and boatmen to carry people up and down or across the river. Some of the wherries, as the boats were called, were covered over against rain and had excellent cushions. Here was obviously a more comfortable way of getting about than walking or driving in the streets as Dekker pictured them.

A good water supply is essential to the health of a town and the convenience of the housewives. But only the very rich had water piped into their homes. London depended on its wells, and the importance of these is shown by the London place-names which record the presence of springs, such as Camberwell and Clerkenwell, and of streams such as Holborn and Tyburn. (The "born" or "burn" are forms of "bourne", meaning a "rivulet".) The water from the springs was carried in pipes, or conduits as they were called, to places where there were public taps. Here came people with the tankards mentioned by Dekker to fetch water for their homes; those who could afford to avoid that labour bought water from men known as cobs who earned a living by carrying it round.

Just before the end of Shakespeare's life London got its first properly organized water-supply through the wisdom and energy of a man from Wales, Sir Hugh Myddelton. He tapped the streams north of London to make what was called, and still is called, the New River. It can be seen to-day at Canonbury and further up. This feat of construction brought a fresh supply right into north London at Islington and the headquarters of the present Metropolitan Water Board keep the title of New River Head. Myddelton had a hard struggle to finance his scheme but he had the backing of King James I, known as the learned fool, but showing no folly in this matter. The New River began at last to pay its way and was a great contributor to the health of London since well-water in a town with no drains could easily become tainted and dangerous.

Despite its many primitive conditions, London was much esteemed as a city and admired for its beauty. The poets sang of the "silver Thames" which had not got its murky look of to-day. The swans were numerous and salmon came up for the citizens to catch. The wherries and the elegant barges brought life and colour to the river and every Londoner was living close to open country and could go fowling or fishing, riding and shooting within a mile or two of his home.

London was gay with the costumes of those who could afford splendour. Shakespeare several times mentioned taffeta, a thin silk, usually of bright colour. This he contrasted with "honest kersey", woollen cloth named after Kersey in Suffolk, strong and warm stuff for the garments of the poor. When dressed for a great occasion, the ladies were radiantly but heavily clad, with ruffs round their necks and large padded sleeves to their bodices, which were tightly drawn in at the waist. The skirts were the hooped farthingales, which were as cumbrous as a crinoline, and must have made getting in and out of a coach very difficult. They had elaborate headdresses or tires (Shakespeare once lodged with a tire-maker). In a packed room in summer, all must have been very hot. It is little wonder that Bacon advised the spraying of scent in crowded assemblies, since the males too were heavily laden.

*Three engravings from* The Manner of Crying Things in London, *1599 (?) showing a mender of chairs carrying cane for the purpose, a woman selling cheese and cream, and a toy-seller.*

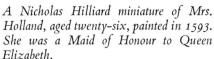

*A Nicholas Hilliard miniature of Mrs. Holland, aged twenty-six, painted in 1593. She was a Maid of Honour to Queen Elizabeth.*

*An Elizabethan woman's coif, embroidered with an intricate and delicate design.*

*A gentleman's glove, finely embroidered.*

The men of fashion had highly decorated gorgets to cover the chest, fine skirted coats, and short trousers, which look very substantial to our eyes. Beautifully decorated gloves were constantly worn. Shakespeare's patron, the Earl of Southampton, was painted thus with his armour beside him, a plumed helmet and a breast-plate. They did not think it effeminate to wear jewels and they made great use of pearls, which were obtained at the mouths of English rivers. Raleigh wore pearl earrings and a row of pearls on his fur-lined coat. Even shoes were jewelled for town wear. So the man who went about his work in kersey and leather had plenty to admire and perhaps envy in the street and on the river.

32

For their amusement, the people did not have organized sport played before big crowds, as we have now. A kind of cricket had been in existence for many years, and Shakespeare mentions football, but one cannot imagine a Stratford team going off to play for a Midland Cup. The countryside had its assemblies for all kinds of racing and athletics. There was a notable meeting for such games at Dover's Hill in the Cotswolds, and Shakespeare speaks of a greyhound being "out-run" there. Boys and men had the rural sports of swimming, fishing, hawking, and hunting. Shakespeare had bowls often in mind. Deer were shot with bow and arrow, and the Queen was quite an expert at this. But gunpowder was replacing archery, and Shakespeare wrote of birds "rising and cawing at the gun's report". If it is true that he was a poacher of deer in his youth, he must have killed his prey with bow and arrow, as the "gun's report" would call attention to his trespass.

In the country towns there were plenty of chances for the people to enjoy plays brought by touring actors. The noblemen in those times liked to have their own companies of players, but naturally did not need them all the time. So the actors went round the country, finding eager audiences, and making enough to pay for their keep. There was a regular flow of these teams through Stratford; if schoolboys could get into the performances—and we can be sure they did their best to do so—Shakespeare could have seen companies carrying the names of the Earls of Worcester, Leicester, and Warwick and of several other lords during the years of his schooling. In addition there was an abundance of home-made theatricals and masquerades. In the early summer there were May Day revels, dancing round the decorated Maypole, and "Whitsun

*Football was played in Elizabethan times. The clothes seem rather bulky and warm for a strenuous game.*

C

*Richard Burbage (1568–1619). He played many of Shakespeare's leading parts. He and Edward Alleyn were the greatest actors of the age. (Dulwich College.)*

Pastorals''; later, the end of sheep-shearing and of the harvest had their jollities.

Stratford had an annual pageant of St. George and the dragon. At Christmas-time and New Year there were groups of enthusiasts who carried "The Mummers' Play" from farm to farm and expected to earn their supper. This too was about St. George, and it survived almost into our time. There is a lively description of it in Thomas Hardy's novel, *The Return of the Native.*

It is a fair guess that seeing the professional actors of the lords' companies during their visits to Stratford prompted Shakespeare to take a chance in a theatrical career. If he went to London in 1587, he would find the people who liked this kind of thing fascinated by the actor Alleyn as he delivered the resounding poetry of a young writer from Cambridge named Christopher Marlowe. The players, despite the opposition of the Puritans, were becoming more and more popular, and so were able to prosper. The early professional, money-making playhouses included the famous Globe Theatre, built by Shakespeare's own company, the Lord Chamberlain's Men, in 1599.

These theatres were partly open to the sky, but a section of the stage was covered, and so were the galleries which surrounded the stage and the exposed arena in front of it. Here there were no seats, and the entrance fee for standing room was a penny. The covered seats cost several pence more and for a chair on the side of the stage sixpence was charged. It is very difficult to translate these sums into their modern equivalents. Multiplying by twenty or even thirty seems fair since a man who earns ten or fifteen pounds a week now got about ten shillings then, and could bring up a family on that. So paying a penny to see a play meant quite a lot to him.

The plays were written by men of talent coming down from the Universities, like Marlowe, or by men who had begun as actors, like Shakespeare. They sold

34

planities siue arena.

Ex obseruationibus Londinensibus
Johannis De Witt

The Swan Theatre, where Shakespeare and his company played in 1596-97. This is a copy of a drawing made by a Dutch visitor, de Witt, who may have been working from memory. It gives only a rough idea of the theatre of the time, but shows the projecting stage and galleries.

whole five-act play to the players for about five pounds and had no more share in the profits. The people who did best were the actors who were also sharers in the company. The Hired Men, as the minor players were called, only got nine or ten shillings a week, and the Boy Players, who played the girls' parts since no women were allowed on the stage, about the same. The Actor-Sharers had to carry the risk of building or hiring a theatre, buying plays and costumes, and putting on the performances. If these proved popular, they could do quite well, and that was how Shakespeare made enough to acquire his fine house in Stratford and land as well. We think of him as the supreme poet, but it was not the poetry that paid.

The audience was of all kinds, from the Queen down to the "groundlings"—that is, those who paid a penny to stand. Their taste was for robust acting in plays with plenty of violent action, battle-scenes, and bloodshed. But they liked the sound of splendid words and poetry too, and could relish a love-scene written in the finest verse. There was much appreciation of the exquisite tragedy of young love, *Romeo and Juliet*. The public wanted anything that glittered and was colourful. Sometimes the audience was noisy and paid more attention to cracking nuts and eating apples than to the voices of the players. But there were also tributes paid by foreign visitors to the rapt attention which the players could command. The standard of acting was evidently high since when the English companies toured in Europe they were generously praised.

It is strange to us that those who were keen patrons of the plays written with rare beauty of language could also enjoy the filthy spectacles to be seen in Paris Garden, next-door to the South Bank theatres. The fanciers of the ring in which bulls and bears were baited by dogs, with mutilation and slaughter of the dogs as well as torment of their victims, were not just the "roughs and toughs" of the town. The Queen and her courtiers were attenders at the Garden and its gory displays.

The bears had their teeth broken short, so that the dogs launched at them were in less danger than they might have been. But even so Shakespeare speaks of the mastiffs running "into the mouth of a Russian bear and having their heads crushed like rotten apples". It is evident that Shakespeare himself was no lover of this entertainment. He sympathized with the "head-lugged bear" and the mastiffs. He must have hated the other sights—of dogs tossed by the maddened bulls, of boys sent into the ring whipping a blinded bear and risking its furious lunges at them, and of an ape put on a horse which the dogs chased madly galloping round the arena until the ape fell off and was savaged.

Yet the poetry of Viola and Orsino was being spoken to admiring crowds next-door to Paris Garden, whose odious performances the Swiss traveller Platter described in detail, adding that the place had an evil smell. Shakespeare's world was one of astonishing contradictions. It mingled blood and beauty, the roars and screams of tortured animals with the tender music of the lutes and viols and with as subtle a melody of words as the English language has ever known.

*A viol, a favourite Elizabethan musical instrument.*

*A gittern, a medieval form of a guitar, converted, perhaps in Elizabethan times, to be played with a bow. It carries the coat of arms of Queen Elizabeth and the badge of Robert Dudley, Earl of Leicester, who is said to have given it to the Queen.*

The English then were a very musical nation. We know that their composers and players were famous and welcomed abroad, as well as much esteemed at home. There is a great deal of music in the land to-day, but nearly all of that is recorded and relayed by radio or record-player. The "do-it-yourself" way is not so common. The Elizabethans had to make their own music or go without.

It is an odd coincidence that one of the renowned musicians of that time was named John Bull. Our idea of John Bull is of a heavy, beevish, rustic type; this image, that is taken to typify Britain, was made up in the eighteenth century. We cannot imagine him enjoying a delicate air or anxious to join in the singing of a glee. The real John Bull, whom Shakespeare must have heard of and perhaps met, was so valued a composer that the Queen called him back from Europe fearing that other nations might capture and keep his artistry. His portrait makes him look rather Italian, and not nearly so Anglo-Saxon as his name.

There was music everywhere. Even those who distrusted all the arts because of their Puritan religion gathered in great numbers to sing psalms and hymns. This was often happening round Paul's Cross in London. Instead of magazines, musical instruments were provided for those waiting in barbers' shops. People sang or played while being ferried across the river. There was a custom of singing "catches" or "rounds", as Sir Toby Belch and his revelling companions do in the comedy *Twelfth Night*. One of these "rounds" for several voices which has remained a favourite to this day, "Three Blind Mice", was devised in Shakespeare's time. In the home all members of the household were expected to take a part in singing of this kind. It was considered disgraceful to be unable to do so. The noblemen kept resident musicians and singers in their mansions. Francis Drake insisted on taking five singers from Norwich with him on one of his voyages. No doubt they had other jobs to do. But he wanted sailors who could sing, and sing well.

There was plenty of music in the theatres. Summoned to the play by a trumpet, the audience expected brass and drums for the battle-scenes and fine rendering of the

The Bull by force In field doth Raigne Bull by Skill Good will doth Cayne

John Bull (1563–1628), one of the most famous Elizabethan composers. The skull and hour-glass symbolise death and the brevity of life, though in fact the portrait was painted when the composer was 28 and he lived for a further 39 years.

A detail of the remarkable painting, "Sir Henry Unton", that depicts scenes from his life. This is a wedding feast at which an orchestra plays in the foreground while children perform a masque. Note that the male guests are wearing hats at table. It was painted about 1590.

songs inserted in the plays. The treble voices of the Boy Players were useful for this, and there are several allusions in Shakespeare to the nuisance caused by the breaking of a treble's voice; it is stated in the text that one of his loveliest lyrics, "Fear no more the heat o' the sun," had to be spoken and not sung for that reason.

The best composers of the time were Dowland, Byrd, and Morley. Morley composed the charming airs for two of Shakespeare's most famous songs, "O mistress mine" in *Twelfth Night* and "It was a lover and his lass" in *As You Like It*. The poet himself continually praised the pleasure of true harmony. He was a tolerant man and ready for new things, but I think that jazz would have horrified him, as well as all the musicians of that age. A word commonly used then of the listeners was "ravished". Harmony enchanted and ravished them. It was regarded as one of the principal elements of a good life.

The most commonly enjoyed instruments were the lute whose strings were played with the finger and the viol for which a bow was used. The guitar was then called the "bandora", which has given us our word "banjo". The place of our piano was taken by the harpsichord and virginal. Queen Elizabeth was an expert performer on the latter.

The courtiers were devoted to what was called "masquing", and very large sums of money were spent on these revels, especially in the reign of King James I and his Danish Queen Anne, a devotee of all gaieties. The expenditure went on costumes,

38

settings, and the hire of professional musicians. The masque was played and danced by amateurs; it was a stately kind of charade in which women could appear as well as men. They often impersonated ancient gods or mythical figures, with sumptuous costumes and elaborate scenery. The text, supplied by poets as a rule, did not greatly matter; it was the appearances, the dancing, and the music that were enjoyed. Marriages were celebrated with masques of this kind and for one of these in 1606, staged after a wedding and before royalty, we have the number of musicians required. That was thirty-eight to which a choir of "chapel voices" was added.

It was therefore true of Queen Elizabeth that she would have music wherever she went. And the same was the case with her people whether they were townsmen and their wives sitting in an alehouse or its garden, or countryfolk dancing round a Maypole or ending the labours of a sheep-shearing and a harvest with glees and madrigals. As was said, those who would have nothing to do with masquing or merry-making and called the Maypole a "stinking idol", liked to be community singers and to hold meetings for holy chanting. Caliban's lines in *The Tempest*

the isle is full of noises,
Sounds and sweet airs, that give delight and hurt not

was true of Shakespeare's England.

*A horn book used in school. It was so called because the printed lesson, in this case the Lord's Prayer, was covered in a sheet of transparent horn to protect it. The horn book was also called the absey book (A, B, C book), which Shakespeare mentioned in his play, King John.*

*The schoolroom in Stratford Grammar School which the young William Shakespeare must have attended.*

There is a general idea that most of the population in Shakespeare's world were illiterate. This may well be an exaggeration, since in his plays the servants can read and write. Maria, described as the Lady Olivia's "woman" in *Twelfth Night*, says that she can write just like Her Ladyship, and Mopsa, the country shepherdess in *The Winter's Tale*, declares that she loves a ballad in print and wants one bought for her. Mistress Quickly, the inn-keeper, could write out a bill. Simply because there was no system of compulsory education for all (and there was to be none until 1870), we must not assume a general ignorance of letters.

The habit of signing a document by making one's mark is no proof that the person signing in this way could not write his name if he troubled to do so. We know much less about the girls' education than the boys', but there must have been some lessons at a dame's school or in the home. How else did Mopsa come to read ballads in print? We know that in the towns there was a big popular demand in the streets for ballads which were written to give news and views of big events or of crimes and punishments. There were no newspapers, and the ballad-mongers helped to let people know what was going on through the sale of their printed sheets.

The boys who went to a grammar school, like that at Stratford, were strictly and narrowly educated. Latin was the principal subject after they had learned to read and write in their own language. This they did with the aid of a horn book, known as an "absey" (A, B, C). It was a printed alphabet sheet covered with transparent horn to keep it from being tattered and destroyed. One that has been preserved has the Lord's Prayer printed underneath for reading practice. This could be used in the home, which was the "prep" school of those times, since the entrant to a grammar school had to know his letters and write his name before he could get in.

Schooldays were long. They began at six in the morning in summer and seven in winter. Breaks came at nine for breakfast and at eleven for dinner. Lessons began again at one and lasted till five. There were two half-holidays a week and forty days of full holiday in the year. Discipline was severe and corporal punishment much employed. The strokes of a cane or birch were called "jerks". The allusions to schools, schooling, and schoolmasters in Shakespeare's plays suggest that he did not enjoy himself. The masters are made laughable and the pupils go "towards school with heavy looks". But it is evident that he was well grounded in Latin.

He did not, as far as we know, go on to a University, although he must have had abundant talent and Oxford was only forty miles away from his home. Universities were not for young men and women: they were more like advanced schools. Francis Bacon went to Trinity College, Cambridge, before he was thirteen. The Earl of Essex entered the same College at ten and was a Master of Arts at fourteen. The sons of the

*A wooden doll, c. 1600, typical of those sold at Bartholomew's Fair.*

*Sir Francis Bacon (1561–1626), essayist, lawyer, philosopher and statesman, who was one of the most remarkable writers of his time.*

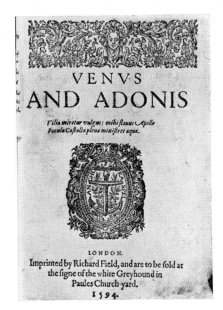

*The title page of the first of Shakespeare's works to be published. Field, the printer, had come to London from Stratford.*

rich did not as a rule go to school, but had private tutors at home until they went to the University. Sir Philip Sidney, who was sent to the new school for boys at Shrewsbury before going on to Oxford, was an exception. But it was not only the sons of the wealthy who went to the University. There were endowments for poor scholars. The dramatist Marlowe, who was the son of a shoe-maker, went from the King's School at Canterbury to Corpus Christi College at Cambridge.

Passing by the disputed question of how many could read, it is certain that those who could did so eagerly. The craft of printing was less than a hundred years old in England when Shakespeare was a boy. But once Caxton had set up his press at Westminster the desire for books created a wide and rapid expansion of the printing trade. So books were no rarities in Queen Elizabeth's reign. The country clergyman, John Bretchgirdle, who baptized the infant Shakespeare, had quite a large library, and left volumes in Latin as well as English to the sons of a Stratford draper, one of the tradesmen's class, to which Shakespeare's father belonged. Stratford was not an illiterate town.

One of the successful London printers came from there. That was Richard Field, the son of a tanner, who went to London, became apprenticed in the craft, succeeded to his master's business, and printed Shakespeare's first published work in 1593. That was the long love-poem called *Venus and Adonis*. This must have been a good bargain for Field, since the poem was very popular and went into many editions. The London printers multiplied and their special district, known as Little Britain, was just north of St. Paul's; they also set up presses in Fleet Street.

43

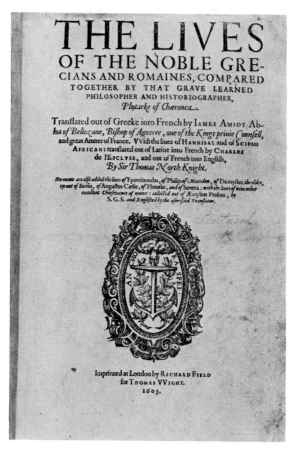

*Of the books most used by Shakespeare there stand out two, the* Lives *of Plutarch and the* Chronicle *of Holinshed, the former used as the basis of the Roman plays, the latter for that of the histories,* Lear, Macbeth *and* Cymbeline. *With both these works Shakespeare must have been extremely familiar. Left, the title-page of the first English translation of Plutarch published in 1603.*

With the increase of printing, books became plentiful, and rich men had libraries well stored with books brought from Europe, as well as those coming off the English presses. The great Bodleian Library at Oxford was founded by Sir Thomas Bodley, who had acquired the books owned by the Earl of Essex, many of them seized by the Earl during his successful naval raid on Cadiz. If Shakespeare could use the library of his patron, the Earl of Southampton, that would give him source-books for the plots of his plays. As he seems always to have lived in lodgings he could not house a big collection of his own, but he must have had the standard English histories of his time written by Hall and Holinshed and a translation of the lives of the great figures in ancient Greek and Roman life, written by Plutarch, since he used these so much for his historical and classical plays.

Half of his plays were printed separately in small books known as "quartos" because each page was a quarter the size of a large folded sheet. When his work was collected and edited by his fellow-actors, Heminge and Condell, seven years after his death,

44

the thirty-six plays were issued in one volume, known as the "First Folio". A folio sheet was a large, unfolded one.

A quarto volume could be bought for about sixpence. The actor Alleyn paid fivepence for a copy of Shakespeare's Sonnets in the year of its publication. It is supposed that about a thousand copies of the First Folio were printed, and priced at a pound; that was then a very large sum, but the first edition must have sold well, since another, the Second Folio, was needed nine years later.

Romances, or what we call novels, were beginning to be read. One of these was *Rosalynde*, written by Thomas Lodge; from this Shakespeare took the plot of *As You Like It*. There was no hesitation then about borrowing of this kind. But the habit of reading for light entertainment was still small. The printers were kept busy issuing poetry and a wide range of informative books, telling people how to cook, garden, ride, play musical instruments, and keep accounts. It was a world full of those who wanted to get upwards and onwards in their careers and to widen their sports and pleasures. Little Britain and Fleet Street were pouring out volumes to meet the demand.

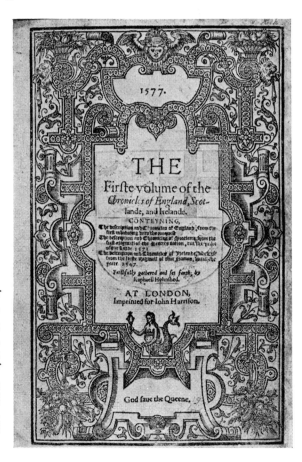

*The title page of the first edition of Holinshed published in 1577, elaborately ornamented with the "strap-work" design widely favoured by Elizabethan craftsmen. The book contains the History of Macbeth including an account of the meeting of "Makbeth" and "Banquho" with the three witches that compares almost word for word with Shakespeare's dialogue. The play Macbeth was not completed until 1606.*

*A surgical instrument.*

*A medical practitioner's signboard of 1623. The panels surrounding the figure of the doctor show his various activities including drawing teeth, amputation, bleeding and treating a tumour.*

Life moved at the gallop then. We hear much of youth and its problems now. For the Elizabethans there was hardly any youth. Their teenagers were men and women. The Earl of Essex, Master of Arts at fourteen, was Master of the Horse at eighteen. That was a very high military command. Those who went to see the first performances of *Romeo and Juliet* would not have been surprised to learn that the young bride was only fourteen. The Boy Players were at work when they were ten, and soon had long parts, like that of Juliet, to play. Driving so rapidly into adult life, people wore themselves out early. To be forty was regarded as being old. Shakespeare died at fifty-two, and so did the leading actor of his company, Richard Burbage.

The practice of medicine was carried out by some able men, who had studied in the universities of Europe and acquired all the knowledge then available. But they had nothing like the experience, the equipment, and the drugs that we have now. An aching tooth was pulled out by the barber. It could not be filled and there were no replacements. A toothless old age was taken for granted; that is implied in Shakespeare's famous passage about the Seven Ages of Man. He frequently alluded with disgust to the stinking breath of the mob, which indicates that dental decay was general.

With dangerous drinking water, no sanitation, and the recurring ravages of plague, the prospect of a ripe and serene old age was only for the fortunate. Anaesthetics were unknown. The sufferings of mothers in childbirth must have been intense, and these sufferings were often in vain. Infant and child mortality was high and parents took the loss of some of their children as natural and inevitable. Shakespeare was the third child of his parents. Two daughters had died in infancy, and another girl died later at the age of eight. Shakespeare's only son died when he was eleven. He wrote of the quick passing of "golden boys and girls". "Life is but a flower" was the constant theme of the poets. That "brief life is here our portion" was an opinion more natural to those times than our own.

The dirty, close-packed town life of the poor was full of crime and cruelty. We ourselves cannot boast of having ended robbery with violence; far from it. The Elizabethans applied ruthless penalties which we are too humane to employ. The death sentence was incurred by quite petty offences, such as minor theft, as well as highway hold-ups. But that did not prevent London from being full of thieves and swindlers, whose methods of tricking the simple were described in detail by writers of the time. There is an account of how touring actors were robbed by a rogue called Ratsey. This scoundrel was caught later on and hanged. But most of the criminals got away with their plunder since the members of the Watch, as the police were called, were amateurish and incompetent. In Shakespeare's plays they are butts and their folly provides comic parts for the clowns.

Executions were numerous and provided public spectacles relished by the crowd. The condemned man was driven to Tyburn, which was near to the present Marble Arch, in an open cart with a rope round his neck, and there he was hanged, to the general satisfaction. If his crime had been treason (and it was quite easy to be falsely accused of that) he was disembowelled while hanging from the gibbet and his body was cut into quarters. Platter recorded that "rarely does a law-day pass in London in all the four sessions without some twenty to thirty people, men and women, being hanged". Vicious women were publicly flogged. There was plenty for the bloodthirsty to enjoy, and not only among the carnage in Paris Garden.

We have to strike a balance between the savage, sordid life of Shakespeare's world and the sparkling vitality and love of beauty in words, music, and decoration which have made the period fascinating to all who read about it. Wealth was used with taste, and not only for display. The Puritans scolded this eagerness to be elegant, but it was

*A surgical instrument. Both this illustration and the one on the opposite page are reproduced from a medical book published in 1612.*

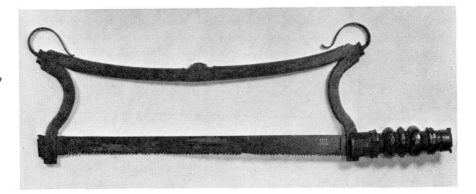

*A large sixteenth-century amputation saw.*

not all vanity. The dandies were devotees and defenders of the poets, players, and musicians. Without their championship of fine things in fine houses our legacy of fine writing would be much smaller.

It is surprising to us that the vast discrepancy in wealth between the owners of great possessions and the poorer people was not more resented. Conspiracies and attempted rebellions came from religious, political, or personal causes. There was no big uprising of the populace striving to increase their standard of life. A probable cause of this was the feeling that it was a world of opportunity, in which the energetic and inventive could make their way without interference by the State or crushing taxation.

A new sort of prosperity was coming among those who developed new ideas in manufacture and commerce. The industrial adventurers were called "projectors", and many of their projects increased the amenities of all as well as the fortunes of a few. The New River was a good example of this. Some people thought that investing money for gain was wrong, but it was pointed out that trade would not increase without an incentive of this kind. So the "putting out" of money, as it was termed, was more and more practised. The actors were themselves investors in their own theatres, often with excellent results in the profits made as well as in the quality of the plays and spectacles they could offer to the public.

It was an active, inventive, remunerative, and fairly free world for those who worked hard and used their brains. It was also a world with a great deal of laughter to relieve its uglier aspects. The intellectuals loved a display of wit as well as beauty of language; others were delighted by the broad humours of the comedians on the stage and the antics of clowns and mountebanks at the frequent fairs, of which St. Bartholomew's was the greatest in London. It is impossible to see or read the plays of the period, and not Shakespeare's only, without realizing that most of the people were able to forget their troubles amid their mirth. Foreign visitors to London praised it for its buildings, its river, and its pageantry, and were impressed by the sight of a confident nation which was well on its toes and had a light in its eyes.